A CHAPTER

FROM THE AUTOBIOGRAPHY

OF

MR. THURLOW WEED.

Stage Coach Traveling Forty-Six Years Ago.

A CHAPTER

FROM THE

AUTOBIOGRAPHY

OF

MR. THURLOW WEED.

STAGE-COACH TRAVELING FORTY-SIX YEARS AGO.

REPRINTED
FROM "THE GALAXY" OF APRIL, 1870.

ALBANY:
PRINTING HOUSE OF CHARLES VAN BENTHUYSEN & SONS.
1870.

STAGE-COACH TRAVELING

FORTY-SIX YEARS AGO.

VERY few of our citizens possess information, other than traditional, of the mode of travel between Albany and the western part of New York, even as late as 1824. Those who step into a railway car at Albany, at seven o'clock in the morning, and step out to get their dinner in Rochester, at two o'clock P. M., will find it difficult to believe that, within the memory of by no means the "oldest inhabitant," it required, in muddy seasons of the year, seven nights' and six days' constant traveling in stages to accomplish the same journey.

And yet, that was my own experience in April, 1824. We left Albany at eight o'clock in the evening, and traveled diligently for seven nights and six days. The road from Albany to Schenectady, with the exception of two or three miles, was in a horrible condition; and that west of Schenectady, until we reached "Tripes" or "Tribes Hill," still worse. For a few miles, in the vicinity of the Palatine Church, there was a gravelly road, over which the driver could raise a trot; but this was a luxury experienced in but few localities, and those "far between." Passengers walked, to ease the coach, several miles each day and each night. Although they did not literally carry rails on their shoulders, to pry the coach out of ruts, they were frequently called upon to use rails for that purpose. Such snail-paced movements and such discomforts in travel would be regarded as unendurable now. And yet passengers were patient, and some of them even cheerful, under all those delays and annoyances. That, however, was an exceptional passage. It was only when we had "horrid bad" roads that stages "drew their slow lengths along."

But stage-coach traveling had its bright as well as its dark aspects. I will endeavor to reverse the scene. Take, for illustration, an early September day. The coach leaves Rochester after breakfast in the morning, if with a full complement, nine passengers inside and two on the box with the driver. At Pittsford and Mendon and Victor, where the stage stops to change the mail and water the horses, a lady or boy, but usually a lady, comes with a basket of peaches, of which the passengers are invited to partake, but for which they are not permitted to pay, except in thanks. At Canandaigua, a beautiful village, then rejoicing in a greater number of distinguished men than are now to be found in any interior city of our State, we get dinner; and the dinners at "BLOSSOM'S," as all who ate them will remember, were dinners indeed. To prove what I say in relation to the distinguished residents of Canandaigua, I will name GIDEON and FRANCIS GRANGER (Postmasters-General under MADISON, in 1812, and HARRISON, in 1840), NATHANIEL W. HOWELL, JOHN GREGG, JOHN C. SPENCER, MYRON HOLLEY, OLIVER PHELPS, DUDLEY MARVIN, HENRY B. GIBSON, JARED WILSON, MARK H. SIBLEY, &c.; two or three of whom are almost certain to become our fellow passengers. PETER TOWNSEND and JOSEPH EVERINGHAM are highly intelligent young merchants from New York city, who have lately established themselves there. GEORGE H. BOUGHTON, subsequently a State Senator and Canal Commissioner from Lockport, was then a merchant's clerk at Canandaigua. There were others, if not wits themselves, the occasion of wit in others. To this class *Spienceer Chopin*, who mawkishly affected the Scottish accent, and Judge ATWATER belonged. When a prisoner was on trial for an attempt to break open Judge ATWATER's mansion, the Judge himself became a witness. His manner was deliberate, and his language pedantic. He stated that he was awakened at the "witching time" of night, by an unusual noise; that on listening attentively he became satisfied that burglars were attempting to enter his castle; that he assumed an erect position on his bed, and at that particular moment "Bose" spoke. DUDLEY MARVIN, the prisoner's counsel, rose, and with quaint solemnity said: "May it please the court, I am not a little surprised that the witness, himself an eminent jurist, who on other occasions graces the seat which your honor now occupies, should so far forget the law of evidence and the gravity of a charge which affects the liberty of my client, as to proceed in this most irregular manner. No person knows better than my distinguished friend, Judge Atwater, that the testimony he is giving is wholly irregular. If it is important that this court and jury should know what 'Bose' saw and heard on the night of this alleged burglary, 'Bose' himself must take the witness's stand. 'Bose' is no stranger; we all know him as sagacious, observing, and vigilant." This produced an irresistible outbreak, involving the audience, the bar, the jury, and the court, in roars of laughter. And when, after an interval of several moments, order was attempted to be restored, it was found quite impracticable to proceed, and the case was actually laughed out of court. Here we find as fellow-passengers, Mr. Wadsworth or Major Spencer, of Geneseo, Mr. Ellicott or Mr. Evans, of Batavia, Mr. Coit, Major J. G. Camp, or R. B. Heacock, of Buffalo, General Porter, of Black Rock, General Paine, of Ohio, and others, who arrive in the stage from Buffalo.

Leaving Canandaigua, we are driven through a charming series of agricultural landscapes to Geneva, sixteen miles, where we have a view of its beautiful lake, a lake not unlike or unworthy of its equally beautiful namesake in Switzerland. At Geneva either Joseph Fellows, a land agent, Henry Dwight, a banker, or Mr. PROUTY, a merchant, is pretty sure to join us. From Geneva to Waterloo, four miles, seems but a turn of the kaleidoscope, and the distance from Waterloo to Seneca Falls is gotten over in no time. At Seneca Falls the chances are at least one to two that we are joined by Colonel MYNDERS, who is going over to Auburn to visit his friend Judge MILLER.

The drive over Cayuga Bridge, more than a mile in length, was always pleasurable and interesting. Some one would remark how much it was to be regretted that a lake so large should be of so little practical value, not being used for purposes of navigation or inhabited by fish of any value.* Looking north, we discern the Montezuma marshes, where COMFORT TYLER failed to manufacture salt; while a southerly view, though you do not actually see, directs your attention to the beautiful village of Aurora, near the head of the lake, then the residence of JETHRO WOOD, HUMPHREY HOWLAND, EBENEZER BURNHAM, EPHRAIM MARSH, &c., and now of the MORGANS, wealthy and reputable merchants; also of WILLIAM H. BOGART, the veteran Senate reporter, and the "Sentinel" letter-writer of the New York *Courier and Enquirer* and New York *World*, a gentleman who has been for more than thirty years about the Legislature without becoming obnoxious to charges of improperly interfering with legislation. Here, too,

* Cayuga Lake is now inhabited by excellent fish, and navigated by steam and canal boats.

resides, in palatial splendor, HENRY WELLS, who, more than thirty-five years ago, "solitary and alone," with a single carpet bag, founded and inaugurated what is now the American Merchants' Union Express Company. I first knew Mr. WELLS more than forty years ago, teaching boys "how not" to stutter. My only son was one of his pupils. But though Mr. WELLS cured others, he could not cure himself. Mr. WELLS still lives to enjoy the fruits of his prosperity, and may he live long and happily, for I have known few men more worthy of prosperity. A few miles from Aurora, beautifully situated upon the lake shore, is a valuable farm, purchased many years ago by MOSES H. GRINNELL, one of the merchant princes of the city of New York, for some relatives, who reside there.

When finally over the long bridge, we discuss THOMAS MUMFORD, a lawyer residing at the end of it, and Colonel GOODWIN, a worthy tavern keeper, midway between Cayuga Bridge and Auburn. And during the many years that I was accustomed to travel in stages between Cayuga and Auburn, I cannot remember the time that some one of the passengers did not amuse the coach by relating an incident that occurred to Mr. JOHN C. SPENCER several years before. The coach drove up to the hotel at the end of the bridge, to water the horses. It was a dark, rainy, cold evening. The stage was full inside and out. A lady, closely veiled, came to the steps, who was, as the keeper of the hotel said, very anxious on account of sickness in the family where she resided, to get to "GOODWIN'S" that evening. The passengers said it was impossible, as there were already nine of them inside. But Mr. SPENCER, prompted by his sympathies or his politeness, as it was but four miles, thought a lady ought not to be refused a passage, and offered, if she chose to accept it, a seat on his lap. The offer was accepted, the lady took her seat, and the stage dashed off. At "GOODWIN'S Tavern," where the lady got out, a light was brought to enable her to find a part of her luggage, and when she removed her veil, a very ebony colored individual of the female gender was revealed, to the consternation of Mr. SPENCER, and the amusement of the other passengers!

At Auburn we rest for the night, having made sixty-four miles. In the evening, the magnates of the village would drop into the hotel bar-room to gossip with the stage passengers. There were no sitting or drawing rooms at hotels in those days; nor could a single lodging room, or even single bed, be obtained. In country inns, a traveler who objected to a stranger as a bedfellow was regarded as unreasonably fastidious. Nothing was more common, after a passenger had retired, than to be awakened by the landlord, who appeared with a tallow candle, showing a stranger into your bed!

The leading men of Auburn were Judge MILLER, JOHN H. and E. S. THROOP (since Governor), NATHANIEL GARROW, PARLIAMENT BRONSON, &c. WILLIAM H. SEWARD had commenced his professional and public life at Auburn one year before. Genial "KIT" MORGAN was at Yale College.

In the morning, the stage was off between daylight and sunrise. The passengers refreshed themselves, enjoyed a view of refreshed and invigorated nature, to which the rising sun soon began to impart light and life. The canal was attracting business and population; the stage had just begun to run over the Northern or New Turnpike, leaving the villages of Skaneateles, Marcellus, Onondaga, West Hill, Onondaga Hollow, and Jamesville, on the line of the old turnpike, to a process of decay which has rendered them almost obsolete. I ought to have remarked that, at Auburn, passengers always dreaded an acquisition to their number in the person of Mr. WOOD, who, weighing some four hundred pounds, and inconveniently broad across the shoulders and transom, made the coach every way uncomfortable. As a sleeper and snorer, he would compare favorably with any one of "the seven." For ten or fifteen miles there was little of outside interest to talk about. In passing through Camillus, the richly cultivated farms and large granaries of the brothers SQUIRE, DAVID and NATHAN MUNRO, attracted attention, and some one would be pretty sure to remark that "the MUNROS not only owned the best farms in the town themselves, but had mortgages on all their neighbors' farms," which was true. Our approach to stage houses and post offices was announced by the blowing of a tin horn or trumpet, with more or less skill, by the driver. This drew together a crowd of idlers, with this difference between New York and many parts of Europe — that instead of beleaguering the coach with imploring appeals for charity, our visitors would generally present us with some choice fruit.

At Syracuse, twenty-five miles from Auburn, we breakfasted. Syracuse then, as now, was a marvel in the suddenness and rapidity of its growth. And here, *my* story came in. I had worked in the Onondaga furnace in 1811 and 1812, and remembered having gone through what was now the flourishing village of Syracuse, with six or seven thousand inhabitants, when it was a tangled and almost impenetrable swamp, thickly inhabited by frogs and water-snakes. Indeed, the swamp foliage was so thick, and darkened the atmosphere to such an extent, that the owls, mistaking day for night, could be heard hooting. Upon the locality over which the now large and beautiful city of Syracuse has extended, there was, in 1811, but one human habitation; that was "COSSETT'S Tavern," near the site of the present Syracuse House. At the western boundary of the swamp, on the creek which empties into the lake, there was a small grist mill and two log cabins. In September, 1812, soon after the declaration of war with England, a letter was written by the Secretary of the Navy (Dr. EUSTIS), showing how lamentably that Cabinet Minister's geographical education had been neglected.

Captain WOOLSEY, who commanded the United States brig "Oneida," was ordered to proceed from Oswego to Onondaga, there to take on board the cannon ball manufactured at the Onondaga furnace for the Government.*

And this incident reminds me of another, and one which at this day will be regarded almost as incredible as the order of the Secretary of the Navy; for, while ships were unable to ascend the rifts and falls of the Oswego River, salmon did make their way from Lake Ontario through the Oswego River and the Onondaga Lake into the Onondaga Creek, and were killed two miles south of the city of Syracuse. I remember well of being attracted, in the Spring of 1811, to WOOD'S mill-dam, by torches flitting below the dam in the creek. Arriving at the spot, I saw Onondaga Indians with clubs watching for and killing salmon, as they were seen making their way over the rifts. I joined in the sport, and came out with a fine salmon as my share of the spoils. I carried my salmon to Mr. JOSHUA FORMAN (then a lawyer in Onondaga Hollow, subsequently the inventor and father of Syracuse), for which he paid me a large, round, bright silver dollar; this being my exact recollection of a coin which was of more value to me then, and was a source of higher gratification than the receipt of thousands of dollars in after years. I then

* This is paralleled by the supply of tanks for *holding fresh water,* sent from England for the English vessels of war built at Kingston during the war of 1812.

spoke of Judge ASA DANFORTH, indicating his residence in the Hollow, who was the first white inhabitant of Onondaga county. This led me to speak of ELEAZAR WEBSTER, a white boy captured by the Onondaga Indians, during the Revolutionary War, in the Mohawk Valley. Young WEBSTER, as he grew up, like JOSEPH among the Egyptians, grew in favor with the Indians. Before white inhabitants reached that part of the State, young WEBSTER had been made a chief of the Onondaga nation, and had married a daughter of an old chief, and received as her bridal portion a mile square of the lands belonging to the Onondaga nation. Mr. WEBSTER continued to reside with his Indian wife and to act as a chief of the tribe long after the county was organized and settled by white inhabitants. In 1808 or 1809, Governor TOMPKINS appointed Mr. WEBSTER agent of the State, to receive and disburse the money paid annually to the Onondaga nation. He was subsequently appointed a Justice of the Peace and Judge of the County Court. After the death of his Indian wife, in 1810 or 1811, he married an intelligent and reputable white lady, with whom he was living happily when I last heard of him, with children by both wives growing up in harmony and affection. Mr. WEBSTER was a man of good sense, good habits, and good character, enjoying alike the respect and confidence of his white and red neighbors and acquaintances.

After breakfast, we leave Syracuse and drive rapidly on to Manlius Square, where passengers were always warmly welcomed at the stage house by its host, Col. ELIJAH PHILLIPS, one of six brothers, all men of mark, of whom I shall have occasion to speak hereafter. Mrs. PHILLIPS, an estimable lady, was the daughter of Judge DANFORTH, and the first white child born in the county of Onondaga. Manlius was the residence of AZARIAH SMITH, a merchant remarkable for his enterprise, activity, industry, and integrity. He had a greater and more varied capacity for business than any other man I have ever known. He was many years Supervisor of the town, doing not only his own business thoroughly, but the business of almost every member of the Board of Supervisors. As a member of the Legislature, his time and talents were severely taxed. Though Chairman of the Committee on Claims and a member of two or three other working committees, while discharging all their duties promptly, he found leisure and was always ready to do the work of fifteen or twenty idle or incompetent members from other counties. He was also an administrator or executor of such of his neighbors as left property requiring attention.

If, as the horn blew for passengers to take their seats, JOHN MEEKER did not, at the last moment, make his appearance, some one would express their surprise at his absence. JOHN MEEKER was an extraordinary man. He owned and cultivated three or four of the largest farms in the towns of Pompey, Tully and Preble. He had stores, not only in those three towns, but in Fabius, Homer, and Manlius, managed under his personal supervision by clerks. He always sold produce at the lowest prices for cash, or on approved credit. He paid the highest prices in cash or goods for black salts, and for pot and pearl ashes. He had an ashery as an appendage to each of his stores. He went frequently to Albany and New York to purchase goods. He was an uneducated man, with the appearance and in the costume of a common farmer. With all these establishments, spreading over so large a surface, it will be apparent that Mr. MEEKER was a man of extraordinary business talents; but when people have so many irons in the fire, some of them will inevitably burn, while others as inevitably get cold; and in the end, like many others who overtrade, JOHN MEEKER "came to grief."

In passing through the north corner of the town of Pompey, Pompey Hill would be suggested as the residence of HENRY SEYMOUR, a capable Canal Commissioner (and father of ex-Governor HORATIO SEYMOUR). VICTORY BIRDSEYE, an eminent lawyer and equally eminent statesman, also resided at Pompey Hill. There, too, SAMUEL S. BALDWIN, a flash lawyer and fast gentleman, resided. He married JULIANA, a daughter of Judge PETER W. YATES, who enjoyed a wax-work celebrity in TROWBRIDGE'S Museum as the "Albany beauty." Judge YATES, when, in the early years of the present century, he resided at Albany, occupied, if he did not erect, the mansion subsequently owned by JAMES KANE, and successively occupied by Governors TOMPKINS, CLINTON and SEWARD.

From Manlius we passed through Eagle Village to Canaseraga Hollow, where the chances were in favor of picking up General J. J. M. HURD, of Cazenovia, a merchant with agreeable manners, who went to Albany and New York to purchase goods as often as was convenient, he evidently fancying that part of his business. In ascending a hill, eastward, the stage stops at the suggestion of some passenger, who invites the others to go with him a few rods from the road and look at an immense petrified tree, lying upon the surface, and perfect, except where it had been broken to gratify the curiosity of visitors, each of whom, of course, carried away a specimen. A few miles further east brought us to Quality Hill, where passengers always promised themselves enjoyment at the expense of a most polite, obsequious, and good-natured tavern keeper. Mr. WEBB (for that was his name), was truly an original. In deportment if he had lived in London, and been a dancing master instead of keeping a hotel on Quality Hill, he might have rivaled Turveydrop; in his zeal to preserve the credit of his house, and his tact in concealing the meagreness of his larder, CALEB BALDERSTONE might have taken lessons with advantage from our host of Quality Hill. Here, in all probability, one of the numerous family of SPENCERS would be added to our list of passengers, among the survivors of whom I only know Mr. JULIUS SPENCER, a most worthy man and an essential fixture in the Albany office of the New York Central Railroad. Proceeding eastward, and after rising Breakneck Hill, we came to the Oneida Castle, the residence of the Oneida tribe of Indians. These Indians, long surrounded by white inhabitants, had emerged from their savage habits and customs, and were enjoying the advantages of civilization. These advantages consisted in loafing about taverns and groceries, and in drinking bad whiskey. Full two-thirds of the tribe had ceased to hunt, or to fish, or to cultivate their lands, than which none more fertile were to be found in the State. Large numbers of both sexes were idling about the tavern, all or nearly all of them endeavoring to sell some trinket for the purpose of buying whiskey. This process of demoralization went on until the few who did not die prematurely were induced to emigrate beyond the Mississippi. After leaving the Castle, the passengers would talk of the devotion of Rev. Mr. KIRKLAND to the Oneida Indians, of the eloquence of SHENANDOAH, one of their aged chiefs, and of a French officer, Colonel DE FERRIER, who married an Indian wife at Oneida Castle, and whose sons and daughters were well educated ladies and gentlemen; and this topic would scarcely be exhausted when we were driven into the village of Vernon, where we always changed horses.

In Vernon itself there was nothing especially remarkable. The hotel was kept by a Mr. STUART, whose sons and grandsons were persons of more or less consideration in different parts of the State for many years afterward. From Vernon to Westmoreland was but a few miles. The hotel at Westmoreland was kept by Mrs. CARY, a widow lady, with six or seven attractive and accomplished daughters, who, as far as propriety allowed, made the hotel pleasant for its guests. These young ladies, quite well known by intelligent and gentlemanly stage passengers, were sometimes irreverently designated as "Mother CARY's chickens." In this, however no disrespect was intended, for, though chatty and agreeable they were deservedly esteemed, and all, "in the course of human events," were advantageously married.

From Westmoreland we were driven rapidly through New Hartford into Utica, seventy-two miles from Auburn. This was the end of our second day's journey. But, for the accommodation of those who preferred a night ride, a stage left Utica at nine P. M. Those to whom time was important took the night line. We, however, will remain over. Utica is now no "pent-up" place. But as I have, in an earlier part of this narrative, given a brief account of its highly intelligent citizens, we will pass on. And departing early the next morning, the first object that attracts the attention is the pleasantly-situated mansion and fruitful surroundings of Colonel WALKER, an aide-de-camp of General

WASHINGTON in the Revolutionary War. A few miles further on, as we cross the Mohawk river, the humble farm house pointed out is the residence of Major General WIDRIG, who was ordered, with his division, into the service during the war of 1812. But that Major General was found to be so lamentably deficient in penmanship, orthography, and arithmetic as to render his resignation as proper as it proved acceptable. Further on, in the town of Schuyler, I pointed to a lofty, two-pronged pine tree, under which, in September, 1814, the regiment to which I belonged, commanded by Colonel MATTHEW MYERS, of Herkimer, ate its first ration; and where, to my great satisfaction and as grateful remembrance, the Quartermaster of the regiment, GEORGE PETRIE, then a merchant, subsequently a member of Congress, and now a venerable clerk in the General Post Office at Washington, appointed me his Quartermaster's Sergeant.

Before reaching the ancient village of Herkimer, we were driven over the fertile and celebrated German Flats, nearly a thousand acres of which were owned by Judge JACOB WEAVER and Colonel CHRISTOPHER BELLINGER. They were neighbors, and, unless drawn into political discussion, warm friends. During a sharply contested election in the spring of 1814, while at the polls, these old gentlemen collided. The conversation waxed warmer and warmer, until they were about to engage in a personal conflict. Friends, however, interfered in season to avert what both in their cooler moments would have lamented. Subsequently, they shook hands and calmly reviewed their cause of quarrel. "You ought not," said Colonel BELLINGER, "to have lost your temper." "And you ought not," said Judge WEAVER, "to have called me a British tory." I only did so," said Colonel BELLINGER, "after you called me a French Jacobin." "And then," said Judge WEAVER, "you not only called me a British Tory again, but said that I rejoiced when *Ox*enburgh was taken, and I couldn't stand that." Many amusing anecdotes were told of Judge WEAVER'S early life, when he was a merchant and trading with the Indians. In purchasing furs, as the story goes, his hand, placed on the scale opposite the fur, weighed half a pound, and his foot a pound. His accounts were kept on boards, in chalk. One of his neighbors, Mr. HARTER, in settling an account, found himself charged with a cheese. Being a farmer, and making not only cheese for his own table, but cheese he was in the habit of selling at his store, he asked an explanation. Judge WEAVER, priding himself upon his accuracy, was impatient with all who disputed his accounts. But Mr. HARTER appealed to his reason and common sense to show how improbable, if not impossible, it was, that he who made cheese for sale should have been a purchaser. This perplexed the Judge, who, after thinking and talking for a long time, was unwilling under the circumstances, to press his neighbor to pay for a cheese, and equally unwilling to admit an inaccuracy in his bookkeeping. The question was finally laid over till the next day, in the hope that the Judge might be able to verify the integrity of his books, or boards. On the following day, when Mr. HARTER appeared, the Judge met him in jubilant spirits, exclaiming, "It is all right; I remember all about it now." "But," said his neighbor, "you don't mean to say that I bought the cheese!" "No, no," said the merchant; "it was not a cheese, but a grindstone; and I forgot to put the hole in it!" In Judge WEAVER'S mode of bookkeeping, a circular chalk mark represented a cheese, while the same mark, with a dot in the centre, converted it into a grindstone. Those two splendid farms have long since, by a very common process, been melted into one. General CHRISTOPHER P. BELLINGER married the daughter of Judge WEAVER, and thus inherited both farms. General BELLINGER, a very worthy man, with whom I served in the Legislature of 1830, and who has been for fifty-seven years my intimate friend, is still living. Here resided also Major WEBER, a wealthy German farmer, who was with us at Sackett's Harbor. Though a second officer in our regiment, he found the service anything but pleasant. I have an order, now in my possession, directing me to take possession of a building for a regimental hospital, no word of which with more than two syllables is spelt right, and which is signed "J. P. WEBER, Gomadand."

On one occasion, when Sir James Yeo's fleet appeared off Sackett's Harbor, for the purpose, as was supposed, of landing troops, and our regiment, with others, was ordered to a point directly opposite the fleet, Major Weber was in a greatly excited state, constantly asking subordinates and privates if they supposed the British intended to land, and complaining of the injustice of pushing militia instead of regular troops into such an exposed position. "It was not," he said, "on his own account that he was unwilling to be crowded into battle where he was sure to be killed, but on account of the feelings of his wife, who was in delicate health." He inquired also, "whether he couldn't resign his commission." Fortunately, however, for the Major, after a couple of hours of trepidation and suspense the fleet made sail and soon disappeared.

From Herkimer to Little Falls, seven miles, there were no particular attractions; nor indeed was there much of interest at the Falls, a small village, with a valuable water-power, nearly unavailable on account of its being owned by Mr. Edward Ellice, a non-resident Englishman. Mr. Ellice was a large landholder in this State and in Canada. It was my privilege, in 1861 and 1862, to become well acquainted with him in London. He enjoyed the reputation of being the most influential commoner in England. He was a man of giant frame and intellect. He was one of the oldest members of Parliament, and had been once or twice a member of the British Cabinet. He died at his country-seat in Scotland in 1864, in the eighty-third year of his age. The London residence of Mr. ELLICE, in Arlington street, looking into St. James's Park, now improved and modernized, was occupied by HORACE WALPOLE a century ago, and in it many of his celebrated letters were written.

From Little Falls we come after an hour's ride to a hill, by the bank of the river, which several years before, General SCOTT was descending in a stage, when the driver discovered, at a sharp turn near the bottom of the hill, a Pennsylvania wagon winding its way up diagonally. The driver saw but one escape from a disastrous collision, and that, to most persons would have appeared even more dangerous than the collision. The driver, however, having no time for reflection, instantly guided his team over the precipice and into the river, from which the horses, passengers, coach, and driver were safely extricated. The passengers, following General SCOTT's example, made the driver a handsome present as a reward for his courage and sagacity. We dine at East Canada Creek, where the stage-house, kept by Mr. COUCH, was always to be relied on for excellent ham and eggs, and fresh brook trout. Nothing of especial interest until we reach SPRAKER's, a well known tavern, that neither stages or vehicles of any description were ever known to pass. Of Mr. SPRAKER, senior, innumerable anecdotes were told. He was a man without education, but possessed strong good sense, considerable conversational powers, and much natural humor. Most of the stories told about him are so JOE-MILLERISH that I will repeat but one of them. On one occasion he had a misunderstanding with a neighbor, which provoked both to say hard things of each other. Mr. SPRAKER, having received a verbal hot shot from his antagonist, reflected a few moments and replied, "FERGUSON, dare are worse men in hell dan you;" adding, after a pause, "but dey are chained." Mr. SPRAKER used to say that "when his son DAVID was a boy, he thought he would make a smart man; but he sent him to college, and when he came back from Schenectady he didn't know enough to earn his living."

At Canajoharie a tall, handsome man, with graceful manners, is added to our list of passengers. This is the Hon. ALFRED CONKLING, who in 1820 was elected to Congress from this district, and who has just been appointed Judge of the United States District Court for the Northern District of New York by Mr. ADAMS. Judge CONKLING is now (in 1870) the oldest surviving New York member of Congress. The late Hon. SAMUEL R. BETTS, recently United States Judge for the Southern District of New York, was elected to Congress from Orange county in 1815. JOHN CRAMER, of Saratoga, though the senior of Judge CONKLING, being over ninety, was not elected to Congress until 1833.

In passing CONINE'S Hotel, near the Nose, the fate of a beautiful young lady, who "loved not wisely, but too well," with an exciting trial for breach of promise, &c., would be related. Still further east, we stop at FAILING'S tavern to water. Though but an ordinary tavern in the summer season, all travelers cherish a pleasant remembrance of its winter fare; for leaving a cold stage with chilled limbs, if not frozen ears, you were sure to find in FAILING'S bar and dining rooms "rousing fires;" and the remembrance of the light, lively, "hot and hot" buckwheat cakes, and the unimpeachable sausages, would renew the appetite even if you had just risen from a hearty meal.

Going some miles further east, we come in sight of a building on the west side of the Mohawk river, and near its brink, the peculiar architecture of which attracts attention. This was formerly CHARLES KANE'S store, or rather the store of the brothers KANE, five of whom were distinguished merchants in the early years of the present century. They were all gentlemen of education, commanding in person, accomplished and refined in manners and associations. CHARLES KANE resided in Schenectady, JAMES KANE in Albany, OLIVER KANE in New York, ELIAS KANE in Philadelphia, and ARCHIBALD KANE in the West Indies. An incident which occurred there in 1808 is remembered by some of the passengers, who relates it. Some gentlemen, who had been invited to dine there, amused themselves after dinner with cards. In the course of the evening a dispute arose between OLIVER KANE and JAMES WADSWORTH, of Geneseo, a gentleman of high intelligence, great wealth, and enlightened philanthropy, the latter years of whose life were distinguished for zeal and liberality in the cause of normal schools and school district libraries. The quarrel resulted in a challenge, and the parties met before sunrise the next morning, under a tall pine tree, on a bluff behind the store, and exchanged shots, Mr. KANE receiving a slight wound. More than thirty years afterward, I was walking with Mr. WADSWORTH and his son, the late General J. S. WADSWORTH, in Broadway, where he met Mr. OLIVER KANE, with whom young Mr. WADSWORTH exchanged salutations; and observing that his father passed making "no sign," he said, "Don't you know Mr. KANE?" "I met him once," was the laconic reply. Supposing that JAMES had not heard of the duel, when we were alone, I mentioned it to him, to which he replied, laughing, "I knew all about that, but I wanted to draw the Governor out." I had endeavored, several years earlier, to induce Mr. WADSWORTH to accept a nomination for Governor, and thereafter JAMES S. was accustomed to speak to and of him as Governor.

Here Commodore CHARLES MORRIS, one of the most gallant of our naval officers, who in 1812 distinguished himself on board the United States frigate "Constitution" in her engagement with the British frigate

"Guerriere," passed his boyhood. In 1841, when I visited him on board of the United States seventy-four-gun ship "Franklin," lying off Annapolis, he informed me that among his earliest recollections was the launching and sailing of miniature ships on the Mohawk River. On the opposite side of the river, in the town of Florida, is the residence of Dr. ALEXANDER SHELDON, for twelve years a member of the Legislature from Montgomery county, serving six years as Speaker of the House of Assembly. The last year Dr. S. was in the Legislature, one of his sons, MILTON SHELDON, was also a member from Monroe county. Another son, SMITH SHELDON, who was educated for a drygoods merchant, drifted some years ago to the city of New York, and is now the head of the extensive publishing house of SHELDON & Co., Broadway.

The next points of attraction were of much historical interest. Sir WILLIAM and GUY JOHNSON built spacious and showy mansions a few miles west of the village of Amsterdam, long before the Revolution, in passing which interesting anecdotes, relating to the English baronet's connection with the Indians, were remembered. A few miles west of Sir WILLIAM JOHNSON'S, old stagers would look for an addition to our number of passengers, in the person of DANIEL CADY, a very eminent lawyer, who resided at Johnstown, and for more than fifty years was constantly passing to and from Albany. At Amsterdam, MARCUS T. REYNOLDS, then a rising young lawyer of that village, often took his seat in the stage, and was a most companionable traveler. He subsequently removed to Albany, where for more than a quarter of a century he held a high professional and social position.

And now, as the valley of the Mohawk spreads out more broadly, and the eye wanders over fields teeming with the bountiful products of Mother Earth, we come in view of Schenectady, first seen by a graduate of Union, who immediately becomes eloquent in his laudation of Dr. NOTT, whose sermon at Albany against duelling, occasioned by the death of General HAMILTON, is claimed as the greatest effort of the age. Our graduate would then enumerate the distinguished men scattered over the Union who owed their success in life to Dr. NOTT's peculiar mode of lectures and training. Then, as we approached the old bridge across the Mohawk he would tell us how long it had withstood storm and tempest, and how many dark secrets it would disclose if it could talk. Next, he would have a brief history of Mr. GIVENS, the gentlemanly keeper of the hotel in Schenectady, and of his still more gentlemanly son, Major G., who brought back from West Point to Schenectady all the discipline and proprieties, physical and social, of a military education, and who vibrated for half a century between Schenectady and Saratoga, saying and doing polite and civil things to and for everybody. Perhaps allusion might be made to Mr. GIVEN's predecessor in the hotel, only for the purpose of remarking that his daughter, a beautiful and accomplished young lady, rejected wealthy suitors for the sake of the fine person and melodious voice of a music master, preferring, it would seem, musical to circulating notes; concluding, almost certainly, with an account of a phrenological discussion, in which Governor YATES floored his antagonist by saying, "My head is not so long as Governor CLINTON'S, but it is a great deal *ticker*."

From Schenectady to Albany the drive through dwarf pines and a barren soil, the turnpike road ornamented with poplar trees at uniform distances on either side, was tame, and, unless enlivened by conversation, dull. But it was an unusual circumstance to find a stage-coach, with fair weather and good roads, between Rochester and Albany, that was not enlivened by conversation, for there were almost always two or three intellectual passengers. MYRON HOLLEY, for example, with a gifted and highly-cultivated mind, had committed to memory and would recite by the hour gems from the British poets. Mr. GRANGER also had a good memory, and would often, during the evening, recite from BURNS, MOORE and others. RICHARD L. SMITH, a reckless lawyer from Auburn, with his wit and drolleries, would make hours and miles seem short. And there was an unfailing source of fun at every stopping place, in the "gibes and jokes" of the stage-drivers, who, as a class, were as peculiar, quaint and racy as those represented by the senior and junior WELLER in "PICKWICK," as "SAMIVEL" described them—a class of highly-social individuals, who have been driven off the roads and compelled to earn a precarious living by tending pikes and switches, or marrying "vidders," and whose unintellectual successors were engine-drivers and stokers.

The stage drivers of that day lived merry but short lives. The exceptions were in favor of those who, after a few years' experience, married some reputable farmer's daughter on their route, and changed their occupation from stage-driving to farming. This must, I think, have been the case with one of my earliest stage-driving acquaintances. It is but a few weeks since I saw in the papers the announcement of the death somewhere in Tompkins county of "PHINEAS MAPES," aged eighty years. "PHIN MAPES," a rollicking stage-driver at Catskill, is one of my earliest remembrances. In 1803 or 1804, a stage with four live horses was an institution, at least in the admiring eyes of boys. I remember with what a flourish "MAPES" used to dash up to the post office door, and, while Dr. CROSWELL was assorting the mail, how gracefully and gently he would throw his long whip-lash over the backs of the leaders, and how, by the responsive action of their fore-feet, nostrils and ears, they would show how well they understood that he meant it playfully. How well, too, I remember when, in 1810 or 1811, I renewed my acquaintance with this driver at Skaneateles, between which place and Onondaga Hollow he was blowing his horn and cracking his whip and his jokes, quite as popular here as he had been at Catskill. The oldest inhabitants of Catskill and Skaneateles, as well as the few survivors who rode in stages upon the great Genesee turnpike sixty years ago, will remember "PHIN MAPES" pleasantly, from whom, in his best days, DICKENS might have found a "jolly" original for MARK TAPLEY.

THURLOW WEED.

www.ingramcontent.com/pod-product-compliance
Lightning Source LLC
LaVergne TN
LVHW010743120826
845150LV00009B/2283